FIRMLY ON THE ROCK

FIRMLY ON
THE ROCK

•

120

REFLECTIONS

ON

FAITH

•

Debra Herbeck

servant
YOUR TRUSTED CATHOLIC VOICE

Book design by Mark Sullivan
Cover design by Candle Light Studios
Cover photo © Voylodyon | Shutterstock

LIBRARY OF CONGRESS CATALOGING-IN-PUBLICATION DATA
Firmly on the rock : 120 reflections on faith / [collected by] Debra Herbeck.
p. cm.
ISBN 978-1-61636-165-5 (alk. paper)
1. Christianity—Quotations, maxims, etc. 2. Faith—Quotations, maxims, etc. I.
Herbeck, Debra.
BR124.F57 2012
234'.23—dc23
2012013921

ISBN: 978-1-63582-449-0 (softcover)
ISBN: 978-1-63582-483-4 (eBook)

Printed in the United States of America.
10 9 8 7 6 5 4 3 2 1

❈ ❈❁❈ ❈

This book is dedicated to my husband, Peter,
a man of God who believes, lives,
and speaks the truth of our faith

Foreword

Faith is a gift—the greatest gift anyone could receive. Faith gives us a knowledge of what is true and real, a knowledge of what we must do to be saved, a knowledge of what life is all about and how true love is possible, both now and forever. Faith is a trusting, a trusting in One who is absolutely trustworthy, a trusting in One who has made unbreakable promises to us, who has a future full of goodness and love for us. Faith is a joyful obedience, a saying "yes" to the One who loves us, to the One who reveals to us the truth about reality, to the One who has promised never to abandon or forsake us. Faith is a shield that protects us against the fiery darts of the enemy, against the lies that would seek to divert us from the narrow way that leads to life and deceive us into taking the broad way that leads to destruction. Faith enables each of us to walk free and confident in this world and to carry out the mission we have been given, to fulfill the purpose for which we have been created, even in the midst of suffering and disappointment.

Debra Herbeck's collection of quotations on faith is a useful resource for encouraging our faith and helping it to grow.

— 　　　　　　　Dr. Ralph Martin, president, Renewal Ministries
Author of *The Fulfillment of All Desire: A Guidebook for the Journey to God Based on the Wisdom of the Saints*

Introduction

My journey of faith began the day I was born. My Jewish identity was shaped by my traditional grandparents, who were active in the establishment of Israel; by a supportive Jewish community; and by a religious education that culminated in my bat mitzvah at age thirteen. My world was predominantly Jewish, and as a child I thought everyone in the entire world was Jewish!

My life was shattered at fifteen when my older brother died in a car crash one snowy December night. My faith, expressed primarily through customs and traditions, now at best seemed shallow, if not empty. Throughout high school, my confusion, grief, and anger sparked extensive questions about the existence of God and the meaning of life and death. There were no answers that helped me make sense of this tragedy.

Being away from home and studying at a large university brought new focus to my life and broadened my exposure to different kinds of people. My first roommate and other girls in my dorm not only called themselves Christians but claimed to know their Christian God in a personal way. I didn't know anything about Jesus, but I did know their beliefs were off limits to me, a Jew. One day, working on a paper for a literature class, I hesitantly borrowed my friend's Christian Bible, and I was surprised to discover several things. Not only did her Bible contain the Jewish Scriptures, but she actually read this Bible, underlined the words, and wrote her own thoughts in the margins. I couldn't decipher Paul's Letter to the Romans, but one thing was clear to me—these mere words on the pages seemed to speak to my friend and she replied. How could a book filled with stories and myths be alive?

Later that semester, this same friend invited to me to watch a movie in the dorm lounge. If I had known it was called *Jesus of Nazareth,* I never would have gone, but as I watched, something both alarming and intriguing became evident—Jesus was Jewish! As I followed his unfolding story, I was drawn into a life that seemed to hold promise not only for the Jews of his day but also for me. Who was this man, and why did people follow him? I watched as Jesus arrived in Bethany and was greeted by a weeping sister: "Lord, if you had been here, our brother would not have died." How many times had I uttered those same words to a distant, unknown God? I, too, waited at the tomb of Lazarus, now dead four days, as Jesus brought him back to life. "What if," I thought, "death is not the final answer?" I borrowed my friend's Bible and for the first time I read the four Gospels. Late that night I bowed my head and spoke to a God I wasn't even sure existed. "God, if you are real, if Jesus is the Messiah, show me and give me the faith to believe."

That Bible and "prayer" became my constant companions over the next nine months as I examined the claims of Christ and studied messianic prophecies. One night I had a dream in which I was standing in a long dark hallway and a voice called out, "Who do you say I am?"

"I don't know who you are," I responded.

A second time that voiced called to me, and I could see the shape of someone but not the face.

"I don't know, but I want to know," I said.

Finally, as the question was posed a third time, I saw before me the face of Jesus. I awoke from the dream with an understanding that I had made an intellectual assent to the truth about Jesus, but I lacked the faith conviction to make this reality my own. I continued to earnestly seek and to ask for that faith.

A few weeks later I was sitting on my bed in my dorm room, praying the now-familiar line, "Give me the faith to believe." In that moment, the room seemed to fill with a light and presence, and I knew in some inexplicable way that God was there with me in the person of Jesus, who extended his hand and offered me a gift. As I reached out to receive it, I knew it was what I had asked for—the gift of faith. In spite of all the years of never knowing, in my grief, questioning, and unbelief, I instantly knew it was all true, that Jesus was the Messiah, sent to rescue and restore me to relationship with my heavenly father.

May these simple reflections on faith help you seek a deeper faith so that you might personally know the One knocking at the door of your heart.

The

Quotes

1 | *The Reward of Faith*
Understanding is the reward of faith. Therefore, do not seek to understand so that you may believe, but believe so that you may understand.

—*St. Augustine*

2 | *Doubting Thomas*
The disbelief of Thomas has done more for our faith than the faith of the other disciples. As he touches Christ and is won over to belief, every doubt is cast aside and our faith is strengthened.

—*St. Gregory the Great*

3 | *True Image*

Assume that a professional painter is given a commission to paint a picture of the king for those living far away. If he draws a ridiculous and ugly shape on the wood and calls this ungracious picture an image of the king, would it not be likely that the powers that be would be annoyed, on the grounds that the handsome original had been insulted through this bad painting among those who had never seen the king? For people will necessarily think that the original is what the form on the icon shows him to be. If, then, the definition says that Christianity is an imitation of God, the person who has never been given an explanation of this mystery will think that the divine is such as he sees life among us to be, accepting it as a valid imitation of God, so that, if he sees models of complete goodness, he will believe that the divine revered by us is good.

—*St. Gregory of Nyssa*

4 | *Contending in Battle*

Faith means battles. If there are no contests, it is because there are none who desire to contend.

—*St. Ambrose*

5 | *All In*
I may love by halves, I may obey by halves: I cannot
believe by halves: either I have faith, or I have it not.
—*Bl. John Henry Newman*

6 | *Actions Speak Louder Than Words*
Heretics are to be converted by an example of humility
and other virtues far more readily than by any external
display or verbal battles. So let us arm ourselves with
devout prayers and set off showing signs of genuine
humility and go barefooted to combat Goliath.
—*St. Dominic*

7 | *Faith and Love*
For the beginning is faith and the end is love. Now these
two, being inseparably connected together, are of God,
while all other things which are requisite for a holy life
follow after them.
—*St. Ignatius of Antioch*

8 | *Prayer for Trust*
O Lord, whose way is perfect, Help us, we pray, to always trust in your goodness; That walking with you in faith, and following you in all simplicity, we may possess quiet and contented minds, and cast all our care on you, because you care for us; For the sake of Jesus Christ our Lord.

—*Christina Rossetti*

9 | *Authentic Faith*
Jesus offers to all the souls who seek him a face-to-face encounter, to accept him or reject him…. I would be ready to give up my life, but not my faith…. Faith is lacking in the world today because there is too much selfishness and too much striving for financial gain…. Love and faith walk side by side…they perfect each other. Consequently, if faith is to be authentic, there must be a love that gives.

—*Bl. Teresa of Calcutta*

10 | *Encounter with Jesus*
The Christian faith is first and foremost the encounter with Jesus, a Person, which gives life a new horizon.

—*Pope Benedict XVI*

11 | *Help on the Journey*
For there is no man so low, but if he will seek his way with the staff of faith in his hand, and hold that fast, and search the way therewith, and have the old holy fathers also for his guides, going on with a good purpose and a lowly heart, using reason and refusing no good learning, with calling on God for wisdom, grace, and help, that he may well keep his way and follow his good guides, then he shall never fall in peril, but well and surely wade through, and come to such end of his journey as he himself would well wish.

—*St. Thomas More*

12 | *Don't Be a Hypocrite*
Do not have Jesus Christ on your lips, and the world in your heart.

—*St. Ignatius of Antioch*

13 | *Love of Truth*
The fear of falling prey to error must never prevent us from getting to the full truth. To overstep the limit, to go beyond, would be to err through excessive daring; but there are also other errors of timidity which consist precisely in stopping short, never daring to go any farther than half-truths.

Love of truth never goes without daring. And that is one of the reasons why truth is not loved.

—*Henri de Lubac*

14 | *Are You Called?*
God requires a faithful fulfillment of the merest trifle given us to do, rather than the most ardent aspiration to things to which we are not called.

—*St. Francis de Sales*

15 | *God Is Great*
Only a person of very small faith could believe that so great a God has not the power to give food to those who serve Him.

—*St. Teresa of Avila*

16 | *Just Say Yes*
There is only one honest reason why anyone should ever believe anything: because it is true. God is, and God has acted, and God has spoken. Now I must respond. That is the true situation. Do I respond Yes (faith) or No? That is the simple question.

Faith is very simple…. Just say Yes to God. It's the simplest thing in the world.

—*Peter Kreeft*

17 | *The Ultimate Witness*
Martyrdom is the supreme witness given to the truth of the faith: it means bearing witness even unto death. The martyr bears witness to Christ who died and rose, to whom he is united by charity. He bears witness to the truth of the faith and of Christian doctrine. He endures death through an act of fortitude. "Let me become the food of the beasts, through whom it will be given me to reach God."

—*Catechism of the Catholic Church, 2473*

18 | *Profession of Faith*

"Unless I see in his hands the print of the nails, and place my finger in the mark of the nails, I will not believe" (Jn 20:25). Basically, from these words emerges the conviction that Jesus can now be recognized by his wounds rather than by his face. Thomas holds that the signs that confirm Jesus' identity are now above all his wounds, in which he reveals to us how much he loved us. In this the Apostle is not mistaken. As we know, Jesus reappeared among his disciples eight days later and this time Thomas was present. Jesus summons him: "Put your finger here, and see my hands; and put out your hand, and place it in my side; do not be faithless, but believing" (Jn 20:27). Thomas reacts with the most splendid profession of faith in the whole of the New Testament: "My Lord and my God!" (Jn 20:28)....

The Apostle Thomas's case is important to us for at least three reasons: first, because it comforts us in our insecurity; second, because it shows us that every doubt can lead to an outcome brighter than any uncertainty; and, lastly, because the words that Jesus addressed to him remind us of the true meaning of mature faith and encourage us to persevere, despite the difficulty, along our journey of adhesion to him.

—*Pope Benedict XVI*

19 | *Life of Action*

Remember that the Christian life is one of action; not of speech and daydreams. Let there be few words and many deeds, and let them be done well.

—*St. Vincent Pallotti*

20 | *Gift of Faith*

Adored Lord, increase my faith, perfect it, crown it to Your own, Your choicest, dearest gift. Keep me in your fold and lead me to eternal life.

—*St. Elizabeth Ann Seton*

21 | *Friend of God*

At this very moment I may, if I desire, become the friend of God.

—*St. Augustine*

22 | *What Faith Looks Like*

Faith is (readiness) to die for Christ's sake, for His commandments, in the conviction that such death brings life; it is to regard poverty as riches, insignificance and nothingness as true fame and glory and, having nothing, to be sure you possess all things. But above all, faith is the attainment of the invisible treasure of the knowledge of Christ.

—*St. Symeon the New Theologian*

23 | *Endurance Increases Faith*
By allowing me to endure temptations against faith,
the Divine Master has greatly increased in my heart
the spirit of faith.

—*St. Thérèse of Lisieux*

24 | *An Atheist Converts*
Little by little I was led to change my ideas. I was no
longer certain that God did not exist. I began to be
open to Him, though I did not yet have faith. I tried
to believe with my reason, without praying, or praying
ever so little! And then, at the end of my first year in
prison, a powerful wave of emotion swept over me,
causing deep and brutal suffering. Within the space
of a few hours, I came into possession of faith, with
absolute certainty. I believed, and I could no longer
understand how I had ever not believed. Grace had
come to me. A great joy flooded my soul and above all
a deep peace. In a few instants everything had become
clear. It was a very strong, sensible joy that I felt. I tend
now to try, perhaps excessively, to recapture it; actually,
the essential thing is not emotion, but faith.

—*Jacques Fesch*

25 | *Grace Brings Understanding*
Teaching unsupported by grace may enter our ears,
but it never reaches the heart. When God's grace does
touch our innermost minds to bring understanding,
then his word which is received by the ear can sink
deep into the heart.

—*St. Isidore of Seville*

26 | *A Matter of Life and Death*
You never know how much you really believe anything until its truth or falsehood becomes a
matter of life and death to you.

—*C.S. Lewis*

27 | *Father Abraham*
By faith Abraham is called the Father of Faith.
Certainly he deserved this title, because he was only
gradually drawn to know the one true God. He left
family and friends to journey to a strange land. God
has given me so many proofs of his loving providence.
How much more willing should I be to respond to
his invitation to commit myself totally to his plans for
me, even though he leads me in strange ways. Father
Abraham, help me to say yes.

—*Msgr. David E. Rosage*

28 | *We Are in God*
Faith is nothing other than a proper understanding of our being, with true belief and certain trust that we are in God.

—*St. Julian of Norwich*

29 | *The Revelation of God*
For He sent His Son, the eternal Word, who enlightens all men, so that He might dwell among men and tell them of the innermost being of God (see John 1:1–18). Jesus Christ, therefore, the Word made flesh, was sent as "a man to men." He "speaks the words of God" (John 3;34), and completes the work of salvation which His Father gave Him to do (see John 5:36; 17:4).... Moreover He confirmed with divine testimony what revelation proclaimed, that God is with us to free us from the darkness of sin and death, and to raise us up to life eternal. The Christian dispensation, therefore, as the new and definitive covenant, will never pass away and we now await no further new public revelation before the glorious manifestation of our Lord Jesus Christ (see 1 Tim. 6:14 and Tit. 2:13).

—*Dei Verbum, 4*

30 | *At the Heart*

At the heart of silence is prayer. At the heart of prayer
is faith. At the heart of faith is life. At the heart of life
is service.

—*Bl. Teresa of Calcutta*

31 | *Thirst for Faith*

Such awful torments I have suffered and I still suffer
now from this thirst for faith, which is always the
stronger in my soul the greater are my arguments
against it. And yet God sometimes sends me moments
when I am completely at peace; at those times I love,
and I find that I am loved by others, and in such
moments I have composed for myself a symbol of
faith, in which everything for me is lucid and holy.
This symbol is very simple, it is: to believe there is
nothing more beautiful, profound, loving, wise,
courageous and perfect than Christ, and not only is
there not, but I tell myself with jealous love that there
cannot be. What is more, if someone proved to me
that Christ was outside the truth, and it was *really true*
that the truth was outside Christ, then I would still
prefer to remain with Christ than with the truth.

—*Fyodor Dostoevsky*

32 | *See Him*
God's splendor is the source of life, those who see
him share his life. Because he was beyond the reach of
man's mind, incomprehensible and invisible, he made
himself visible, intelligible and knowable so that those
who see and accept him may possess life.

—*St. Irenaeus*

33 | *Sea of Mercy*
All my nothingness is drowned in the sea of Your
mercy. With the confidence of a child, I throw myself
into Your arms, O Father of Mercy, to make up for
the unbelief of so many souls who are afraid to trust in
You.

—*St. Faustina Kowalska*

34 | *The Blind Shall See*
The Bible gives me a deep, comforting sense that
"things seen are temporal, and things unseen are
eternal."

—*Helen Keller*

35 | *Pray with Faith*

Pray! Pray, but with faith—with living faith! Courage, courage! Onward, ever onward!

—*St. John Bosco, shouting encouragement to his boys as he approached death after a prolonged illness*

36 | *When I Can't Pray*

When I am incapable of praying, I want to keep telling Him that I love Him. It's not difficult, and it keeps the fire going.

—*St. Thérèse of Lisieux*

37 | *A Name in the Sand*

Alone I walked the ocean strand;
A pearly shell was in my hand:
I stooped, and wrote upon the sand
My name—the year—the day.
As onward from the spot I passed,
One lingering look behind I cast;
A wave came rolling high and fast,
And washed my lines away.

And so, methought, 'twill shortly be
With every mark on earth from me:
A wave of dark oblivion's sea
Will sweep across the place
Where I have trod the sandy shore
Of Time, and been, to be no more,
Of me—my day—the name I bore,
To leave nor track nor trace.

And yet, with Him who counts the sands
And holds the waters in His hands,
I know a lasting record stands
Inscribed against my name,
Of all this mortal part has wrought,
Of all this thinking soul has thought,
And from these fleeting moments caught
For glory or for shame.

—Hannah Flagg Gould

38 | *Faith Is the Answer*
Ultimately, faith is the only key to the universe. The
final meaning of human existence, and the answers
to the questions on which all our happiness depends,
cannot be found in any other way.

—*Thomas Merton*

39 | *Draw Near*
When the woman suffering from a flow of blood
believed and touched the hem of the Lord's clothing,
her flow of blood dried up. In the same way, every
soul wounded by sin and punished by a flood of evil
thoughts will be saved if it draws near to the Lord in
faith.

—*St. Ammon*

40 | *Wake Up!*
What does it mean, faith is asleep? You have forgotten
it. So what does it mean, to wake up Christ? Waking
up your faith, remembering what you have believed.
So then, recall your faith, wake up Christ; your very
faith will command the waves you are being troubled
by, and the winds of persuasive perversity.

—*St. Augustine*

41 | *A Door*
The outsiders stand by and see, or think they see,
the convert entering with bowed head a sort of small
temple which they are convinced is fitted up inside like
a prison, if not a torture-chamber. But all they really
know about it is that he has passed through a door.
They do not know that he has not gone into the inner
darkness, but out into the broad daylight.

—*G.K. Chesterton*

42 | *The Teacher*
Jesus does not need books or doctors to teach souls.
He, the Doctor of doctors, teaches without the noise
of words. I have never heard Him speak and yet I
know He is in me. At every moment, He guides me
and inspires me.

—*St. Thérèse of Lisieux*

43 | *Purification*

There is no progress in charity without purification of faith. This is exemplified in our Blessed Lady. She was often baffled. She did not understand. She "kept these things in her heart."… Faith must be purified…. After all, we have given our lives to God and yet, so often, he seems so elusive. We long for light and are left in darkness. We long for consolation and find only pain. And faith is sorely tried, because faith ultimately is dependence on and acceptance of God alone.

—*Cardinal George Basil Hume,* O.S.B.

44 | *Weapon of Faith*

Let us carry bravely the shield of faith; with this protecting, whatever the enemy throws can be extinguished.

—*St. Cyprian of Carthage*

45 | *The Habit of Faith*

Faith, in the sense in which I am here using the word, is the art of holding on to things your reason has once accepted, in spite of your changing moods. For moods will change, whatever view your reason takes. I know that by experience. Now that I am a Christian I do have moods in which the whole thing looks very improbable: but when I was an atheist I had moods in which Christianity looked terribly probable. This rebellion of your moods against your real self is going to come anyway. That is why faith is such a necessary virtue: unless you teach your moods "where they get off," you can never be either a sound Christian or even a sound atheist, but just a creature dithering to and fro, with its beliefs really dependent on the weather and the state of its digestion. Consequently one must train the habit of faith.

—*C.S. Lewis*

46 | *Are There Miracles Today?*
You hear people saying sometimes that there are fewer
miracles nowadays. Might it not rather be that there
are fewer people living a life of faith?

—*St. Josemaría Escrivá*

47 | *Walking With Jesus*
Put your hand in His [Jesus'] hand, and walk alone
with him. Walk ahead, because if you look back you
will go back.

— *Dronda Bojaxhiu to eighteen-year-old Gonxha Agnes*
Bojaxhiu, the future Bl. Mother Teresa, as she left home to
begin her life as a missionary

48 | *True Discipleship*

O Lord Jesus Christ, give me the grace to become your true disciple. Let me see ever more clearly that faith in you is not simply a conviction of my mind—but a call to live my life for you and with you....

Let me welcome you into the center of my poor being just as you came to the house of the publican. Let me seek and find you, recognize and serve you in all who suffer. Give me the grace, O Savior of the world, to bring your presence even to your enemies and to persist faithfully in witnessing to them even when I find it painful to do so. Let me be inspired by your martyrs who constantly call us back to you, our only hope and salvation.

—*Fr. Benedict J. Groeschel, C.F.R.*

49 | *Believing Without Seeing*

Faith, in its essence, is believing without seeing....

When we continually "see" the work of God in our life, there is less need for faith. When the perception of blessing or presence is removed, there is an opportunity to exercise faith on a deeper and purer level, which is very pleasing to God and unites us in a deeper way with Him.

—*Ralph Martin*

50 | *Is It Good to Believe?*

Only now can we answer the question of whether it is
"good" for man to believe. And the answer will have
to run somewhat as follows: If God has really spoken,
then it is not only good to believe him; rather, the
act of believing generates those things that in fact are
goodness and perfection for man. Receptively and
trustfully hearing the truth, man gains a share not only
in the "knowledge" of the divine Witness, but in his
life itself.

—*Joseph Pieper*

51 | *Endurance Produces Faith*

By allowing me to endure temptations against faith,
the Divine Master has greatly increased in my heart
the spirit of faith.

—*St. Thérèse of Lisieux*

52 | *Come and See*
It is not easy to walk in faith, in total belief in the
Trinity; in the love of the Father; in the sustaining,
warm, divine love of the Son; in the strange, incredible
love of the Holy Spirit who is both Wind and Fire....

No, it is not easy. But God will give us that faith,
dearly beloved, and we have to continue to pray for it
so that, full of hope, we might love....

During this year, God will quietly "call out" as he
did in the Gospel when someone asked, "Master,
where dwellest Thou?" He will say to you, "Come and
see." And you will have to "step out" and begin your
walk in faith, in hope, and in love. That is the only
way you can reach him.
—*Catherine de Hueck Doherty*

53 | *He Is Seeking You*
In the first place, if a soul is seeking after God, the
Beloved is seeking it much more.
—*St. John of the Cross*

54 | *True Progress*
It is not the actual physical exertion that counts
towards a man's progress, nor the nature of the task,
but the spirit of faith with which it is undertaken.
—*St. Francis Xavier*

55 | *No Problems...Only Plans*

I remember from my time in prison in Ravensbrück,
where so many men and women were killed, that
Betsie and I sometimes walked in the prison grounds
before we were called for registration in the mornings
at 4:30 A.M. Then God performed a miracle. We
experienced His presence so vividly that it was as
if we were talking to one another. Betsie would say
something, then I would say something, and then
the Lord would say something—and both Betsie and
I heard what He said. I cannot explain it, but it was
wonderful. We saw then that even though everything
was terrible, we could rely on the fact that God did not
have any problems, only plans. There is never panic in
heaven! You can only hold on to that reality through
faith because it seemed then, and often seems now, as
if the devil is the victor. But God is faithful, and his
plans never fail! He knows the future. He knows the
way.

—*Corrie Ten Boom*

56 | *Own Your Decision*

Belief is a decision. We can't get away from the fact. "You cannot serve two masters"; from now on you serve God alone or you don't serve God at all. You have only one master now—that is the world's Master, that is the world's Redeemer, that is the world's re-creator. It is your highest honor to serve God…. Your "yes" to God requires a courageous "no" to everything that tries to interfere with your serving God alone, even if that is your job, your possessions, your home, or your honor in the world. Belief means decision. But your very own decision.

—*Dietrich Bonhoeffer*

57 | *Unity and Faith*

I am always touched to see how Jesus links unity and faith together:

"that they may all be one…so that the world may believe."

If Christians are united, this will help others to believe.

Disunity is an obstacle to faith whether it be disunity between individuals, between groups, between churches.

Disunity prevents people from believing the message of Jesus.

—*Jean Vanier*

58 | *Heaven on Earth*

We go to heaven—not only when we die, or when we go to Rome, or when we make a pilgrimage to the Holy Land. *We go to heaven when we go to Mass.* This is not merely a symbol, not a metaphor, not a parable, not a figure of speech. It is real. In the fourth century, St. Athanasius wrote, "My beloved brethren, it is no temporal feast that we come to, but an eternal, heavenly feast. We do not display it in shadows; we approach it in reality."

Heaven on earth—that's reality! That's where you stood and where you dined last Sunday!

—*Scott Hahn*

59 | *Faith in the Unfailing One*

In life and death keep close to Jesus and give yourself into his faithful keeping; he alone can help you when all others fail you....

When you put your trust in men, excluding Jesus, you will find that it is nearly all a complete loss. Have no faith in a reed that shakes in the wind, don't try leaning upon it; mortal things are but grass, remember, the glory of them is but grass and flower and will fall....

If you look for Jesus in everything, you will certainly find him.

—*Thomas à Kempis*

60 | *Keep Me From Drowning*

I will not mistrust him...though I shall feel myself weakening and on the verge of being overcome with fear. I shall remember how St. Peter at a blast of wind began to sink because of his lack of faith, and I shall do as he did: call upon Christ and pray to him for help. And then I trust he shall place his holy hand on me and in the stormy seas hold me up from drowning.

—*St. Thomas More, in a letter from prison to his daughter*

61 | *Live It Out!*

Christian faith is not simply a set of propositions to be accepted with intellectual assent. Faith is a lived knowledge of Christ, a living remembrance of His commandments, and a truth to be lived out. A word is not truly received until it is put into practice. Faith is a decision involving one's whole existence. It is an encounter, a dialogue, a communion of love and of life between the believer and Jesus Christ, the Way, the Truth, and the Life. It entails an act of trusting abandonment to Christ, which enables us to live as He lived, in profound love of God and of our brothers and sisters.

—*Bl. Pope John Paul II*

62 | *Reality, Not Theory*

Confidence in God implies this living faith in the whole message of the Gospel; a faith that is no mere theoretical belief in an objective truth but a vital creed, by whose agency a superior Reality is continually at work informing our lives.

—*Dietrich von Hildebrand*

63 | *The Deep Magic*

It means…that though the Witch knew the Deep Magic, there is a magic deeper still which she did not know. Her knowledge goes back only to the dawn of time. But if she could have looked a little further back, into the stillness and the darkness before Time dawned, she would have read there a different incantation. She would have known that when a willing victim who had committed no treachery was killed in a traitor's stead, the Table would crack and death itself would start working backward.

—*C.S. Lewis*

64 | *The Light of Faith*

In the light of faith I acquire wisdom in the wisdom of the Word, your Son; in the light of faith I am strong, constant and persevering; in the light of faith I hope: it does not allow me to fail on my way. This light shows me the way: without it I should walk in darkness, and this is why I begged you, eternal Father, to enlighten me with the light of most holy faith.

—*St. Catherine of Siena*

65 | *Aim for the Bull's-Eye*

Here is the most important point: find out what God wants, and when you know, try to carry it out cheerfully or at least courageously; not only that, but we must love this will of God and the obligations it entails, even if it means herding swine the rest of our lives and performing the most menial tasks in the world, because whatever sauce God chooses for us, it should be all the same to us. Therein lies the bull's eye of perfection, at which we must all aim, and whoever comes nearest to it wins the prize.

—*St. Francis de Sales*

66 | *Our Teacher*

Christ, like a skillful physician, understands the weakness of men. He loves to teach the ignorant and the erring he turns again to his own true way. He is easily found by those who live by faith; and to those of pure eye and holy heart, who desire to knock at the door, he opens immediately…. He seeks all, and desires to save all, wishing to make all the children of God, and calling all the saints unto one perfect man.

—*Hippolytus*

67 | *Certainty of Faith*

May our faith be strong; may it not hesitate, not waver, before the doubts, the uncertainties that philosophical systems or fashionable movements would like to suggest to us. May our faith be certain. May it be founded on the Word of God; on deep knowledge of the Gospel message, and especially on the life, person, and work of Christ; and also on the interior witness of the Holy Spirit.

—*Bl. Pope John Paul II*

68 | *Let God Act*

There are two peculiar characteristics of pure faith. It sees God behind all the blessings and imperfect works which tend to conceal Him, and it holds the soul in a state of continued suspense. Faith seems to keep us constantly up in the air, never quite certain of what is going to happen in the future; never quite able to touch a foot to solid ground. But faith is willing to let God act with the most perfect freedom, knowing that we belong to Him and are to be concerned only about being faithful in that which He has given us to do for the moment....

Sometimes in this life of faith God will remove His blessings from you. But remember that He knows how and when to replace them, either through the ministry of others or by Himself.

—*François de Salignac de La Mothe-Fénelon*

69 | *The One Truth*

He is not one truth among many. He is the truth about everything that is true. He is the universal and cosmic truth. Everything that is true—in religion, philosophy, mathematics or the art of baseball—is true by virtue of participation in the truth who is Christ. The problem is not that non-Christians do not know truth; the problem is that they do not know that the truth they know is the truth of Christ....

Many people in our world think they have already heard of Jesus Christ, when in fact they haven't. And they haven't because too often Christians present the truth of Christ as though it is but one truth pitted against other truths—"My truth is better than your truth."

—*Fr. Richard John Neuhaus*

70 | *The Feeling of Faith*

If I am not mistaken, when we say that we can't find God and that he seems so far away, we only mean that we can't feel his presence…. Many people do not distinguish between God and the feeling of God, between faith and the feeling of faith—which is a very great problem. It seems to them that when they do not feel God they are not in his presence. This is a mistake. A person…about to suffer martyrdom for God…does not actually think of him but rather of his pain…. Although the feeling of faith may be wanting, he makes an act of great love. There is a difference between…being in God's presence and having the feeling of his presence. God alone can give you the latter. As to my being able to give you the means of obtaining this feeling, it is impossible.

—*St. Francis de Sales*

71 | *Perfect Faith*

Perfect faith is faith, hope and charity embodied in a single act uniting the heart to God and his purpose, becoming one single virtue, one uplifting of the heart to him in complete surrender…. In this state of perfect faith nothing is more certain as far as God is concerned, and for the heart, nothing more uncertain. And in the union of the two, certainty of faith comes from God and from the doubting heart, faith tempered by uncertainty and hope.

—*Fr. Jean-Pierre de Caussade*

72 | *Dazzling Light*

Faith is a light of such supreme brilliance that it dazzles the mind and darkens all its vision of other realities: but in the end, when we become used to the new light, we gain a new vision of all reality transfigured and elevated in the light itself.

—*Thomas Merton*

73 | *Faith and Reason*

When Christian faith is authentic, it does not diminish freedom and human reason; so why should faith and reason fear one another if the best way for them to express themselves is by meeting and entering into dialogue? Faith presupposes reason and perfects it, and reason, enlightened by faith, finds the strength to rise to knowledge of God and spiritual realities. Human reason loses nothing by opening itself to the content of faith, which, indeed, requires its free and conscious adherence.

—*Pope Benedict XVI*

74 | *Faith Never Limits Love*

How glorious our Faith is! Instead of restricting hearts, as the world fancies, it uplifts them and enlarges their capacity to love.

—*St. Thérèse of Lisieux*

75 | *Drifting Away*
If you examined a hundred people who had lost their
faith in Christianity, I wonder how many of them
would turn out to have been reasoned out of it by
honest argument? Do not most people simply drift
away?

—*C.S. Lewis*

76 | *Unceasing Search*
I have sought you and desired to see intellectually what
I have believed, and I have argued much and toiled
much. O Lord my God, my one hope, listen to me
lest out of weariness I should stop wanting to seek
you, but let me seek your face always, and with ardor.
Do you yourself give me the strength to seek, having
caused yourself to be found and having given me
the hope of finding you more and more. Before you
lies my strength and my weakness; preserve the one,
heal the other. Before you lies my knowledge and my
ignorance; where you have opened to me, receive me
as I come in; where you have shut to me, open to me
as I knock. Let me remember you, let me understand
you, let me love you. Increase these things in me until
you refashion me entirely.

—*St. Augustine*

77 | *Forever, Forever, Forever*
The phrase "forever" made St. Teresa of Avila great.
One day, as a child, she set out from Avila with her
brother Rodrigo through the Adaja gate. As they left
behind the city walls, intending to reach the land of
the Moors where they could be beheaded for love of
Christ, she kept whispering to her brother, who was
beginning to get tired, "forever, forever, forever."

Men lie when they say "forever" about things on
earth. The only true, totally true, "forever" is that
which we say with reference to God. This is how you
ought to live your life, with a faith that will help you
to taste the honey, the sweetness of Heaven whenever
you think about eternal life which is indeed "forever."

—*St. Josemaría Escrivá*

78 | *Faithful Heart*
God has given me such a faithful heart that once I
love, I love for always.

—*St. Thérèse of Lisieux*

79 | *Perfect Vision*
Lord grant that I may see, that I may see you, that I
may see and experience you present and animating
all things…. Jesus, help me to perfect the perception
and expression of my vision…. Help me to the right
action, the right word, help me to give the example
that will reveal you best.

—*Pierre Teilhard de Chardin*

80 | *Obedience*
I want to do what you ask of me, in the way you ask,
for as long as you ask, because you ask it.

—*Pope Clement XI*

81 | *Encountering the Mystery*
That transcendent reality, the "mystery" that surrounds
our world, the presence of which we can detect in our
world, is the mystery that Christians call "God." When
we encounter that reality, the human condition seems
lighter, freer, more of an opportunity and less of a
burden; tomorrow seems an occasion for expectation,
not fear. In encountering the mystery of God, we find
liberation, not bondage.

—*George Weigel*

82 | *Never Stop Seeking*
Seek Jesus. Let your life be a continual, sincere search
for Him, without ever tiring, without ever abandoning
the undertaking, even though darkness should fall
on your spirit, temptations beset you, and grief
and incomprehension wring your heart. These are
the things that are part of life here below; they are
inevitable, but they can also be beneficial because they
mature our spirit. We must never turn back, even if it
should seem to you that the light of Christ is fading.
On the contrary, continue seeking with renewed faith
and greater generosity.

—*Bl. Pope John Paul II*

83 | *All Shall Be Well*

This is the great act intended by our Lord God from
eternity, treasured and hidden in his heart, known only
to himself. By this act he will make all things well.
For just as the Blessed Trinity made everything from
nothing, just so will the same Trinity make everything
wrong to be well. And I was overcome with wonder at
this: our faith is grounded in God's word, and whoever
believes in that word will be preserved completely.
Now holy doctrine tells us that many creatures will
be damned. And if this is true, it seemed impossible
to me that everything should be well, as our Lord had
shown me by revelation. And in regard to this I had
no other answer but this: "What is impossible for
you is not impossible for me. I shall honor my word
in everything, and I shall make everything well." So
I was instructed by God's grace to hold steadfastly to
the faith, and at the same time to believe firmly that
everything will turn out for the best. For this great
action which our Lord will accomplish, and in this
action he will keep his word entirely. And what is not
well shall be made well.

—*St. Julian of Norwich*

84 | *Faith Is Spelled R-I-S-K!*
If then faith be the essence of a Christian life,…
it follows that our duty lies in risking upon Christ's
word what we have, for what we have not; and doing
so in a noble, generous way, not indeed rashly or
lightly, still without knowing accurately what we
are doing, not knowing either what we give up, nor
again what we shall gain; uncertain about our reward,
uncertain about our extent of sacrifice, in all respects
leaning, waiting upon him, trusting in him to fulfill
his promise, trusting in him to enable us to fulfill our
own vows, and so in all respects proceeding without
carefulness or anxiety about the future.

—*Bl. John Henry Newman*

85 | *Light in the Darkness*
Keep the light of faith ever burning—for Jesus alone
is the way that leads to the Father. He alone is the
life dwelling in our hearts. He alone is the light that
enlightens the darkness. Be not afraid. Christ will not
deceive us.

—*Bl. Teresa of Calcutta*

86 | *It Is True!*

This was the wretched child who, on December
25, 1886, took himself to Notre-Dame in Paris for
the Christmas liturgy. I was standing in the crowd,
near the second pillar at the entrance to the choir,
to the right of the sacristy. And it was there that the
thing happened that has dominated my entire life.
In an instant, my heart was touched and I believed.
I believed, with such a force of adherence, such a
lightening of my whole being, with so powerful a
conviction and a certitude leaving no room for any
kind of doubt, that ever since then all the books,
reasonings, hazards of a tumultuous life, nothing has
been able to shake my faith, nor, to tell the truth, to
even touch it. I suddenly had a heart-rending sense
of the innocence, the eternal childhood of God, an
effable revelation. In trying, as I have often done, to
recapture the moment that followed this extraordinary
incident, I find the following elements, which seem
to blend in a single light, like an arm stretched out
by Providence to touch, to open at last the heart of a
poor, desperate child: How happy believers are! But
what if this were true? It is true! God exists, he is there,
he is someone, a being a personal as I am. He loves
me, he calls me.

—*Paul Claudel*

87 | *Four Little Words*
"Thy will be done." What a comfort those four little
words are to my soul. I have repeated them until
they are softened to the sweetest harmony. We are in
darkness, and must be thankful that our knowledge is
not needed to perfect Thy work.

—*St. Elizabeth Ann Seton*

88 | *True Friendship*
The love of creatures is deceptive and disappointing,
but the love of Jesus is faithful and always abiding….
He who cleaves abidingly to Jesus shall be made firm
in Him forever.

Love Him, therefore, and hold Him for your friend,
for, when all others forsake you, He will not forsake
you, or suffer you finally to perish….

To be without Jesus is the pain of hell. And to be
with Him is a pleasant paradise. If Jesus is with you
no enemy can grieve you. He who finds Jesus finds a
treasure, better than all other treasures, and he who
loses Him has lost more than all the world. He is most
poor who lives without Jesus, and he is most rich who
is with Him.

—*Thomas à Kempis*

89 | *Confidence in God*
We need confidence in God as a governing faith all along our path, from our first awakening to the moment when we are summoned to the throne of the Judge Eternal: confidence in God, directing and shaping our actions, itself growing apace with our transformation; confidence that makes us speak with the mouth of the Psalmist, "In Thee, O Lord, have I hoped, let me never be confounded."

—*Dietrich von Hildebrand*

90 | *The Chorus of Faith*
Faith…what the writer of the Epistle to the Hebrews called the substance of things hoped for, the evidence of things not seen. Faith that bridges the chasm between what our minds can know and what our souls aspire after; faith which so dwarfs whatever we may consider ourselves to have achieved, or been, that it makes all men—the humblest, the simplest, the most, in worldly terms, foolish—our equals, our brothers; faith which irradiates our inner being and outward circumstances that the ostensible exactitudes of time and measure, of proof and disproof, lose their precision, existing only in relation to eternal absolutes which everything in the universe proclaims, in which all life has its being—the stones and the creatures, the wind and the clouds, height and depth, darkness and light, everything that ever has been, or ever will be, attempted, or done, till the end of time—all swelling the chorus of faith.

—*Malcolm Muggeridge*

91 | *Two Wings*
Faith and reason are like two wings on which the
human spirit rises to the contemplation of truth. God
has placed in the human heart a desire to know the
truth—to know Himself—so that by knowing and
loving God, men and women may also come to the
fullness of truth about themselves.

—*Bl. Pope John Paul II*

92 | *Proclaim Jesus!*
A simple look at the New Testament shows us how far
we are from the original meaning the word "faith" has
in Christianity. What then shall we do in this "post-
Christian" society? Nothing else but what the apostles
and the first disciples did in their "pre-Christian"
society! Proclaim Jesus Christ!

—*Fr. Raniero Cantalamessa, O.F.M.*

93 | *Doing What Pleases God*
Almighty, eternal, just and merciful God, grant us
in our misery that we may do for your sake alone
what we know you want us to do, and always want
what pleases you; so that, cleansed and enlightened
interiorly and fired with the ardor of the Holy Spirit,
we may be able to follow in the footsteps of your Son,
our Lord Jesus Christ, and so make our way to you.

—*St. Francis of Assisi*

94 | *Trust Him*

Faith in God means essentially trusting God. The more we trust Him, the more we know Him; the more we trust Him, the more certain we are that He is real and that He is trustable. The same principle works with human beings: the best way to know them is trust....
Hope in God means trusting His promises. Hope is faith directed to the future.

—*Peter Kreeft*

95 | *Better Late Than Never*

Late have I loved you. O Beauty ever ancient, ever new, late have I loved you! You were within me, but I was outside, and it was there that I searched for you. In my unloveliness I plunged into the lovely things which you created. You were with me, but I was not with you. Created things kept me from you; yet if they had not been in you they would not have been at all. You called, you shouted, and you broke through my deafness. You flashed, you shone, and you dispelled my blindness. You breathed your fragrance on me; I drew my breath and now I pant for you. I have tasted you; now I hunger and thirst for more. You touched me, and I burned for your peace.

—*St. Augustine*

96 | *A Wise Lover*

A strong and faithful lover of God stands unshaken
in all adversities, and gives little heed to the deceitful
persuasions of the enemy. As I please such a lover in
prosperity, so I do not displease him in adversity. A
wise lover does not so much consider the gift of his
lover as he does the love of the giver. He regards more
the love than the gift, and accounts all gifts little in
comparison with his beloved, who gives them to him.
A noble lover does not rest in the gift, but rests in Me,
above all gifts.

—*Thomas à Kempis*

97 | *Look to Him*

Christians are those who, like the thief on the cross,
have turned to him with faith that is more like a
desperate hope and, in listening to his response, have
found the faith that moves mountains. When our faith
is weak, when we are assailed by contradictions and
doubts, we are tempted to look at our faith, to worry
about our faith, to try to work up more faith. At such
times, however, we must not look to our faith but look
to him. Look to him, listen to him, and faith will take
care of itself. Keep looking. Keep listening.

—*Fr. Richard John Neuhaus*

98 | *Just Information?*

Is the Christian faith also for us today a life-changing and life-sustaining hope? Is it "performative" for us—is it a message which shapes our life in a new way, or is it just "information"?… Faith is the substance of hope. But then the question arises: do we really want this— to live eternally? Perhaps many people reject the faith today simply because they do not find the prospect of eternal life attractive. What they desire is not eternal life at all, but this present life, for which faith in eternal life seems something of an impediment.

—*Benedict XVI*

99 | *His Word Is Our IOU*

God does not expect that our faith should be vague or aimless. The faith must be in His Word. This is the strong anchor to which faith must be attached. The believer who has been given a promise from God has an IOU in his hand which he can present to God over and over again: "Father, Thou hast said, 'Give, and it shall be given to you.'" Nobody shall perish who waits on Him!

—*Mother Basilea Schlink*

100 | *Everlasting Joy*

When he says I will see you again and your heart shall
rejoice, he meant: I will see you; I will snatch you from
the jaws of your enemies; I will crown you as victors;
I will prove to you that I was ever with you as you
fought, like a witness. For when would he not see his
own in the midst of their trials, since he has promised
that he will be with them always, even to the end of
the world?... He will see us and our hearts will rejoice,
and our joy no man shall take from us; for this is the
sole reward for those who suffer for God's sake, to
rejoice forever in his sight.

—*St. Bede the Venerable*

101 | *Truly Live Your Faith*

Christians are light for each other and for the rest
of the world. If we are Christians we have to reveal
Christ. Gandhi once said that if Christians truly lived
their Christianity, there would be no Hindus in India.
This, therefore, is what everyone expects from us: that
our Christianity be real.

—*Bl. Teresa of Calcutta*

102 | *Prayer Is the Key*

We may not be able to understand God. We may not
even be able to believe in him. We may be confused by
the mysteries, contradictions, and improbabilities of
faith, and unable to unravel them in our minds. But
we can all pray. It is the one resource that can never
be taken away from us except by the total collapse of
our minds. We may be impotent, penniless, in prison,
bound hand and foot, stricken in all our limbs, unable
to move, blindfolded and gagged. But we can still
pray. It is the last weapon of the weak, the starving, the
helpless, the puzzled, the unsure. Yet, in its own way,
it is the most powerful weapon of all…. "You may not
believe in God, but that does not prevent God from
believing in you. God's existence is independent of
your believing in him." So it makes very good sense for
the unbeliever to pray for faith, just as it makes sense
for the believer to pray for more faith, as I constantly
do. In a way, the prayer for faith is the purest form of
prayer…. Faith in God is the most precious possession
any of us can have, especially if it is strong and healthy
and exuberant. With faith all things are possible,
but without it all other possessions are ultimately
meaningless. So to pray for faith is the most ambitious
of all prayers—you are asking God to give you the key
to everything else.

—*Paul Johnson*

103 | *Sure Footing*
The steps of faith fall on the seeming void and find the rock beneath.

—*Walt Whitman*

104 | *Faith Transforms Fear*
The Catholic faith in Jesus Christ does not deny fear, any more than Jesus denied his fear in that garden on the outskirts of Jerusalem almost two thousand years ago. Faith transforms fear through a personal encounter with Jesus Christ and his cross. In his free and complete surrender to God's will, Jesus took all the world's fear with him onto the cross and offered that fear, along with himself, to God….

The Christian does not live without fear or against fear. The Christian lives beyond fear.

—*George Weigel*

105 | *Be Watchful*
Vigilant faith…not only observes what is necessary for salvation, but it seeks out, it embraces and practices faithfully everything that can bring it closer to its God.

—*St. Francis de Sales*

106 | *Come Meet Jesus*

Faith is not a wish to believe something or a will to believe something contrary to reason. Faith is not living as if something is true. Faith is the acceptance of a truth based on the authority of God's revelation, as manifested in the Church and in Scripture. God alone causes faith in the believer, and faith is not the acceptance of abstract ideas. It is so often said, "Oh, by faith you have to accept a number of dogmas." No! Faith is participation in the life of God. In faith, two persons meet: God and ourselves. Our affirmation of faith does not come because we see a truth clearly. But it comes from a vision of him who reveals that truth— and we know that he cannot deceive or be deceived.

—*Fulton J. Sheen*

107 | *Seeing Into Eternity*

The eyes of the world see no farther than this life, as mine see no farther than this wall when the church door is shut. The eyes of the Christian see deep into eternity.

—*St. John Vianney*

Anxious Times

Dear God, these are anxious times. Tonight for the
first time I lay in the dark with burning eyes as scene
after scene of human suffering passed before me. I shall
promise You one thing, God, just one very small thing:
I shall never burden my today with cares about my
tomorrow, although that takes some practice. Each day
is sufficient unto itself. I shall try to help You, God, to
stop my strength ebbing away, though I cannot vouch
for it in advance.... All that really matters is that we
safeguard that little piece of You, God, in ourselves.
And perhaps in others as well.... We must...defend
Your dwelling place inside us to the last.... I am
beginning to feel a little more peaceful, God, thanks
to this conversation with You.... You are sure to go
through lean times with me now and then, when my
faith weakens a little, but believe me, I shall always
labor for You and remain faithful to You and I shall
never drive you from my presence....

Don't let me waste even one atom of my strength
on petty material cares. Let me use and spend every
minute and turn this into a fruitful day, one stone
more in the foundations on which to build our so
uncertain future.

    —Etty Hillesum, a Dutch Jewish woman in the height
       of the Nazi persecution of the Jews in Holland

109 | *Signs of His Presence*
Perhaps a man is asked to opt with all his might for
authenticity. Perhaps the great thing is to respond,
with as much integrity as he can summon, to the cues.
There are some—in his own consciousness, in his
art, in his world. And there is this great light that has
appeared in the murk, like a morning star. It is there,
silent and glorious.

—*Thomas Howard*

110 | *Suffering Seen Through the Eyes of Faith*
What people have seen in the papers or on television
has not been a man who wants to look brave or
courageous. What they see is a man who believes in
God and whose faith informs everything he does.
Suffering and pain make little sense to me without
God, and my heart goes out to people who feel
abandoned or alone in their greatest times of need. As
a man of faith, I can really speak of pain and suffering
only in terms of their redemptive, salvific qualities.
This does not mean I have not prayed, as Jesus did,
that it might be God's will that "this cup pass me by."
But by embracing the pain, by looking into it and
beyond it, I have come to see God's presence in the
worst situations.

—*Cardinal Joseph Bernardin*

111 | *Faith Is Not Defeated*
Faith is always at a disadvantage; it is a perpetually defeated thing which survives all its conquerors....
This is the definition of a faith. A faith is that which is able to survive a mood.

—*G.K. Chesterton*

112 | *Finding God in the Everyday*
Mrs. Barrett gave me my first impulse toward Catholicism. It was around ten o'clock in the morning that I went up to Kathryn's to call for her to come out and play. There was no one on the porch or in the kitchen....

In the front room Mrs. Barrett was on her knees, saying her prayers. She turned to tell me that Kathryn and the children had all gone to the store and went on with her praying. And I felt a warm burst of love toward Mrs. Barrett that I have never forgotten, a feeling of gratitude and happiness that still warms my heart when I remember her. She had God, and there was beauty and joy in her life....

All through my life what she was doing remained with me.... Mrs. Barrett in her sordid little tenement flat finished her breakfast dishes at ten o'clock in the morning and got down on her knees and prayed to God.

—*Servant of God Dorothy Day*

113 | *Love Them Anyway*
Love even the most abandoned: love whatever faith in
Christ remains in them: if they have lost this, love their
virtues; if these have gone, love the holy likeness they
bear, love the blood of Christ through which you trust
they are redeemed.

—*St. Ignatius of Loyola*

114 | *The Weight of Obedience*
Do you ask, "What is faith in Him?" I answer, the
leaving of your way, your objects, your self, and the
taking of His and Him; the leaving of your trust in
men, in money, in opinion, in character, in atonement
itself, and doing as He tells you. I can find no
words strong enough to serve for the weight of this
obedience.

—*George MacDonald*

115 | *Do I Really Believe?*
God wants my heart to be totally given to the first
love, so that I will really trust God and give everything
away. I'm still not able to do that. I say, "Leave your
father, leave your mother, leave your brother, leave
your sister, leave your possessions, leave your success.
Don't cling to friends. Trust that God will give you all
you need." But do I really believe it?

—*Fr. Henri J. Nouwen*

116 | *Hearing the Call*

Faith is an adherence, not to a tradition or family or tribe, or even nation, it is an adherence of our life and our works to the Will of God as it is revealed to each in the intimacy of conscience.

Conversion consists in responding to a call from God. A man is not converted at the time he chooses, but in the hour when he receives God's call. When the call is heard, he who receives it has only one thing to do: *obey....*

Conversion is light renewed, love of God renewed. The convert is a man who has died and has risen again.

—*Rabbi Israel Zolli*

117 | *Faith and Experience*

Faith, of course, is not readily understandable, which makes it suspect among people who have been educated to value ideas insofar as they are comprehensible, quantifiable, consistent. Like a poem, which, as Mallarmé pointed out, is not made out of ideas but of words, faith does not conform itself to ideology but to experience. And for the Christian this means the experience of the person of Jesus Christ, not as someone who once lived in Galilee but who lives now in all believers.

—*Kathleen Norris*

118 | *Divine Truth*

[I understood now] what it means for a soul to abide
in truth in the presence of Truth itself. In this divine
Truth I have come to know truths of the utmost
importance—far better than if many scholars had
explained them to me.... The truth that I said was
communicated to me is Truth in itself, truth without
beginning or end. From it there spring all other truths,
just as all love springs from this Love and all glory
from this Glory. And compared to the clarity with
which the Lord revealed it all to me, what I have just
said is obscure indeed.

—*St. Teresa Benedicta of the Cross*

119 | *Becoming Saints*

Our flaws are part of His plan to bring forth holiness
in us. He calls; we answer. By responding to His call
with courage and faith, we can become saints.

—*Fr. Michael Scanlan,* T.O.R.

120 | *Darkness*

It is a time of darkness, of faith. We shall not see
Christ's radiance in our lives yet; it is still hidden in
our darkness; nevertheless, we must believe that He is
growing in our lives; we must believe it so firmly that
we cannot help relating everything, literally everything,
to this almost incredible reality.

—*Caryll Houselander*

The
V o i c e s

St. Ambrose (c. 340–397) was a bishop of Milan who became one of the most influential ecclesiastical figures of the fourth century. He was one of the four original doctors of the Church.

St. Ammon (288–350) was an Egyptian hermit in the desert of Nitria.

St. Augustine (354–430) was a bishop in North Africa, a prolific writer, and a doctor of the Church.

St. Bede the Venerable (672–735) was a monk at the Northumbrian monastery of St. Peter. He is well known as an author and scholar and is the only native of Great Britain to achieve the designation of doctor of the Church.

Benedict XVI (b. 1927) began his pontificate in 2005. He is a scholar of the liturgy and previously served as the Vatican's chief doctrinal official.

Cardinal Joseph Bernardin (1928–1996) served as archbishop of Chicago from 1982 until his death and worked diligently for social justice.

Dronda Bojaxhiu was the mother of Agnes Bojaxhiu, better known as Mother Teresa of Calcutta. Dronda often took her children with her when she took food, clothing, or medicine to the poor.

Dietrich Bonhoeffer (1906–1945) was a German Lutheran pastor, theologian, and participant in the German resistance movement against Nazism. He was executed in a Nazi concentration camp in 1945, and his courage, vision, and brilliance are expressed in his bestselling classic, *The Cost of Discipleship*.

Father Raniero Cantalamessa (b. 1934) is a Franciscan Capuchin who was appointed preacher to the papal household in 1980 by Pope John Paul II. He is also a frequent speaker and prolific author.

St. Catherine of Siena (1347–1380) was a philosopher, theologian, and doctor of the church. She worked to bring the papacy of Gregory XI back to Rome from its displacement in France and to establish peace among the Italian city-states. Along with St. Francis of Assisi, she is one of the two patron saints of Italy.

G.K. Chesterton (1874–1936) was a prolific English writer of poetry, plays, journalism, fiction, and Christian apologetics. He is well known for such works as *Orthodoxy* and *The Everlasting Man*.

Paul Claudel (1868–1955) was a French poet, dramatist, and diplomat and often conveyed his devout faith in his writing.

Pope Clement XI (1705–1774) was pope from 1769 to 1774.

St. Cyprian (d. 258) was born around the beginning of the third century in North Africa, where he received a classical education. After converting to Christianity, he became a bishop in 249 and eventually died a martyr at Carthage.

Fr. Jean-Pierre de Caussade (1675–1751) was a French Jesuit priest of the Society of Jesus and a writer known for his work *Abandonment to Divine Providence*, which includes letters addressed to those suffering under different kinds of darkness, desolation, and trials.

Henri de Lubac, s.j. (1896–1991), was a French Jesuit priest and is considered to be one of the most influential theologians of the twentieth century. He became a cardinal of the Church, and his writings and doctrinal research played a key role in the shaping of the Second Vatican Council.

Catherine de Hueck Doherty (1896–1985) was a pioneer of social justice and the foundress of the Madonna House apostolate. She was also a prolific writer and a dedicated wife and mother.

Servant of God Dorothy Day (1897–1980) was an American journalist, social activist, and devout Catholic convert. In the 1930s, Day helped establish the Catholic Worker movement.

St. Dominic (1170–1221) was the founder of the Dominicans, or Order of Preachers (Ordo Praedicatorum). He was known for his heroic sanctity, apostolic zeal, and profound learning. He is the patron saint of astronomers.

Fyodor Dostoevsky (1821–1881) was a Russian writer of novels, short stories, and essays. He is best known for his novels *Crime and Punishment*, *The Idiot*, and *The Brothers Karamazov*.

St. Elizabeth Ann Seton (1774–1821), the first native-born citizen of the United States to be canonized by the Roman Catholic Church, was a wife, mother, and founder of the Sisters of Charity. She is popularly considered a patron saint of Catholic schools.

St. Josemaría Escrivá (1902–1975), the founder of Opus Dei, was canonized by Pope John Paul II, who declared him as "counted among the great witnesses of Christianity."

St. Faustina Kowalska (1905–1938) was a Polish nun and mystic who, after receiving visions of Jesus, introduced the popular devotion to Divine Mercy.

François de Salignac de La Mothe-Fénelon (1651–1715) was a French bishop, theologian, and author.

Jacques Fesch (1930–1957) was a twenty-seven-year-old playboy who was beheaded for the murder of a French police officer following a bungled robbery. While awaiting execution he became a devout Catholic who lived his remaining days in prison as if he were a monk.

St. Francis of Assisi (1181–1226) was an Italian friar and preacher who founded the men's Franciscan Order, the women's Order of St. Clare, and the lay Third Order of St. Francis. He received the stigmata, making him the first person to bear the wounds of Christ's passion. He died in 1226 while chanting Psalm 142: "With my voice I cry to the Lord."

St. Francis de Sales (1567–1622) was a bishop of Geneva and the leader of the Catholic Reformation. His book *Introduction to the Devout Life* became a classic spiritual guide for living an authentic Christian life.

Hannah Flagg Gould (1788–1865) was an American poet.

St. Gregory of Nyssa (c. 335–after 394) was a bishop of Nyssa (in lower Armenia) who wrote effectively against Arianism and other questionable doctrines, gaining a reputation as a defender of orthodoxy. He was a younger brother of Basil the Great.

St. Gregory the Great (540–604) led the Church through a troubled time as the Roman Empire collapsed. He is a doctor of the Church and was known as "the Father of Christian Worship" because of his exceptional efforts in revising the Roman worship of his day.

Fr. Benedict J. Groeschel, c.f.r. (b. 1933) is a retreat master, psychologist, well-known author, and one of the founders of the Franciscan Friars of the Renewal.

Dr. Scott Hahn (b. 1957) is a popular speaker and teacher on a wide variety of topics related to Scripture and the Catholic faith. He is currently a professor of theology and Scripture at Franciscan University of Steubenville and the founder and director of the St. Paul Center for Biblical Theology.

Etty Hillesum (1914–1943) was a Dutch Jewish woman working in Amsterdam during World War II who served Jewish refugees in a Nazi transit camp. She kept a series of journals and recorded her spiritual awakening. She and her family were sent to Auschwitz, where she died at the age of twenty-nine.

Hippolytus (170–235) was the most important third-century theologian in the Church in Rome.

Caryll Houselander (1901–1954) was an artist and prolific author who enjoyed enormous literary success in the 1940s and 1950s.

Thomas Howard (b. 1935) is a highly acclaimed writer and scholar, raised in a prominent evangelical home (his sister is well-known author and former missionary Elisabeth Elliot). He entered the Catholic Church in 1985.

George Basil Hume, o.s.b. (1923–1999), a cardinal, was a monk for nearly sixty years before his appointment as archbishop of Westminster.

St. Ignatius of Antioch (c. 50–between 98 and 117) was the third bishop of Antioch and a student of John the Apostle. En route to his martyrdom in Rome, Ignatius wrote a series of letters which have been preserved as an example of very early Christian theology.

St. Ignatius of Loyola (1491–1556) was a Spanish knight from a Basque noble family who underwent a conversion while recovering from a serious battle wound. He founded the Society of Jesus, or Jesuits, and emerged as a religious leader during the Counter-Reformation.

St. Irenaeus (2nd century AD–c. 202), was a bishop, early Church father and apologist whose writings were formative in the early development of Christian theology.

St. Isidore of Seville (c. 560–636) was a prolific writer and learned man, who was sometimes called "The Schoolmaster of the Middle Ages." He served as archbishop of Seville in Spain for more than three decades.

St. John of the Cross (1542–1591) was a Spanish Carmelite reformer, mystical writer, and doctor of the Church.

St. John Bosco (1815–1888) was the founder of the Salesian Society, dedicated to the care and education of poor and disadvantaged children.

St. John Vianney (1786–1859), the "Curé d'Ars," served humbly as a priest in rural French parishes. He is the patron saint of priests.

Bl. John Paul II (1920–2005) reigned as pope for almost twenty-seven years and played a key role in the fall of communism. He is one of the most beloved popes of the modern era.

Paul Johnson (b. 1928) is an English journalist, historian, speechwriter, and author.

St. Julian of Norwich (1342–1423), a hermit and one of the greatest English mystics, wrote about God's merciful love and compassion.

Helen Keller (1880–1968) was an American author, political activist, and lecturer. She was the first deaf and blind person to earn a bachelor's degree.

Peter Kreeft (b. 1939), a convert to Catholicism, is a professor of philosophy at Boston College and a well-known author and speaker.

C.S. Lewis (1898–1963) was an Irish-born British novelist, academic, lay theologian, and Christian apologist. He is also known for his fiction, especially *The Screwtape Letters* and *The Chronicles of Narnia*.

George MacDonald (1824–1905) was one of the most respected authors of his generation in nineteenth-century Scotland. His writings, more than fifty books, had a significant impact on the conversion of C.S. Lewis.

Dr. Ralph Martin (b. 1935) is the president of Renewal Ministries and the host of the weekly television program *The Choices We Face*. He is the author of the bestselling book *The Fulfillment of All Desire* and the director of graduate programs in the New Evangelization at Sacred Heart Seminary in Detroit.

Thomas Merton (1915–1968) was a Catholic writer, social activist, and Trappist monk of the Abbey of Gethsemani in Kentucky.

Malcolm Muggeridge (1903–1990) was a British journalist, social critic, and author. An avowed atheist, he moved gradually to embrace Roman Catholicism at age seventy-nine.

Richard John Neuhaus (1936–2009) was a prominent Christian cleric (first as a Lutheran pastor and later as a Roman Catholic priest) and writer. He was the founder and editor of the monthly magazine *First Things* and the author of several books.

St. John Henry Newman (1801–1890) was a prolific English author who converted from Anglicanism to Catholicism and became an Oratorian priest and cardinal.

Kathleen Norris (b. 1947) is a bestselling poet and essayist.

Fr. Henri Nouwen (1932–1996) was a Dutch-born Catholic priest and writer who taught at influential universities for almost two decades until he left to join Daybreak L'Arche community in Canada, living and working with the mentally handicapped until his death.

Joseph Pieper (1904–1997) was a German philosopher whose writings were rooted in the teachings of Thomas Aquinas.

Msgr. David E. Rosage (1913–2009) was a prolific writer and the founder and director of Immaculate Heart Retreat Center in the diocese of Spokane, Washington.

Christina Rossetti (1830–1894) was one of the most important poets in nineteenth-century England; she wrote a variety of romantic, devotional, and children's poems.

Fr. Michael Scanlan, T.O.R. (b. 1931) is the former dean and chancellor of Franciscan University of Steubenville and the author of many books on practical wisdom for the Christian life.

Mother Basilea Schlink (1904–2001) founded the Evangelical Sisterhood of Mary in postwar Germany. She wrote prolifically about how to walk the pathway of the cross joyfully.

Servant of God Fulton J. Sheen (1895–1979) was an American bishop and author known for his preaching and especially for his work on television and radio.

St. Symeon the New Theologian (949–1022) was a Byzantine Christian monk and poet who was the last of three saints canonized by the Eastern Orthodox Church. He wrote that humans could experience the Spirit of God directly.

Pierre Teilhard de Chardin (1881–1955) was a French philosopher and Jesuit priest who trained as a paleontologist and geologist.

Corrie Ten Boom (1892–1983) was a Dutch Christian, who with her father and other family members helped many Jews escape the Holocaust during World War II. Her family was arrested on the report of an informant. Corrie and her sister Betsie were sent to Ravensbrück concentration camp, which Corrie survived but her sister did not.

St. Teresa of Avila (1515–1582) was a prominent Spanish mystic, Carmelite nun, writer of the Counter-Reformation, and doctor of the Church. She was a reformer of the Carmelite Order and, along with John of the Cross, was a founder of the Discalced Carmelites.

Blessed Teresa of Calcutta (1910–1997), an Albanian Catholic nun with Indian citizenship, founded the Missionaries of Charity in Calcutta, India, in 1950 and won the Nobel Peace Prize in 1979.

St. Teresa Benedicta of the Cross (1891–1942), also known as Edith Stein, was a German Catholic philosopher and nun. Born into an observant Jewish family but an atheist by her teenage years, she converted to Christianity, was baptized into the Catholic Church, and was received into the Discalced Carmelite Order. In 1942 she was arrested and sent to the Auschwitz concentration camp, where she died in a gas chamber.

St. Thérèse of the Child Jesus (1873–1897), also known as Thérèse of Lisieux, was a French Carmelite nun, mystic, and doctor of the church. One of the most popular saints of the twentieth century, she was canonized less than thirty years after her death at the age of twenty-four and is best known for her "Little Way" to holiness.

Thomas á Kempis (c. 1380–1471) was a late medieval Catholic monk and the probable author of *The Imitation of Christ*, one of the best-known Christian books on devotion.

St. Thomas More (1478–1535), lawyer, scholar, author, and lord chancellor of England, was martyred for his principled faith and is known for his courage and fortitude in the face of death.

Jean Vanier (b. 1928) is a Swiss Catholic philosopher and author and the founder of L'Arche, an international organization that creates communities where people with developmental disabilities and those who assist them share life together.

St. Vincent Pallotti (1795–1850) was the founder of the Pious Society of Missions. He was instrumental in establishing schools, guilds, and institutes that carried the Catholic mission into the very heart of contemporary society.

Dietrich von Hildebrand (1889–1977), a convert to Catholicism, was a German philosopher, theologian, and author.

George Weigel (b. 1951) is a distinguished senior fellow of the Ethics and Public Policy Center. He is a Catholic theologian and author and one of America's leading public intellectuals.

Walt Whitman (1819–1892) was an American poet, essayist, and journalist.

St. Francis Xavier (1506–1552) was a student of St. Ignatius of Loyola and one of the first seven Jesuits. He led an extensive mission into Asia and was influential in the spread of Catholicism, most notably in India, but he also ventured into Japan, Borneo, the Moluccas, and other areas that had not been visited by Christian missionaries.

Rabbi Israel Zolli (1881–1956) was chief rabbi of Rome from 1939 to 1945. After the war, he converted to Roman Catholicism, taking the name Eugenio, the baptismal name of Pope Pius XII.

Sources

1. Augustine, quoted in *Nicene and Post-Nicene Fathers: First Series*, ed. Philip Schaff (New York: Cosimo, 2007), p. 184.

2. Pope Gregory the Great, quoted in *Quotable Saints*, ed. Ronda De Sola Chervin (Oak Lawn, Ill.: CMJ Marian, 2003), p. 86.

3. Gregory of Nyssa, quoted in *The Treasury of Catholic Wisdom*, ed. John A. Hardon (San Francisco: Ignatius, 1995), p. 64.

4. Ambrose of Milan, quoted in *The Power of the Cross: Applying the Passion of Christ to Your Life*, ed. Michael Dubruiel (Huntington, Ind.: Our Sunday Visitor, 2004), p. 112.

5. John Henry Newman, *Discourses Addressed to Mixed Congregations* (London: Longmans, Green, 1906), p. 162.

6. Dominic, quoted in *A Dictionary of Quotes from the Saints*, ed. Paul Thigpen (Ann Arbor, Mich.: Charis, 2001), p. 19.

7. Ignatius of Antioch, quoted in *The Heart of Catholicism Essential Writings of the Church from St. Paul to John Paul II*, ed. Theodore E. James (Huntington, Ind.: Our Sunday Visitor, 1997), p. 63.

8. Christina Rossetti, quoted in *The Flowering of the Soul: A Book of Prayers by Women*, ed. Lucinda Vardey (Toronto: Knopf, 1999), p. 155.

9. Blessed Teresa of Calcutta, quoted in Lush Gjergji, *Mother Teresa: To Live, To Love, To Witness Her Spiritual Way* (Hyde Park, N.Y.: New City, 1998), p. 65.

10. Benedict XVI, *Great Christian Thinkers: From the Early Church Through the Middle Ages* (Minneapolis: Fortress, 2011), p. 71.

11. Thomas More, quoted in Allan K. Jenkins and Patrick Preston, *Biblical Scholarship and the Church: A Sixteenth-Century Crisis of Authority* (Burlington, Vt.: Ashgate, 2007), p. 115.

12. Ignatius of Antioch, quoted in Michael A.G. Haykin, *Rediscovering the Church Fathers: Who They Were and How They Shaped the Church* (Wheaton, Ill.: Crossway, 2011), p. 41.

13. Henri de Lubac, *Paradoxes of Faith* (San Francisco: Ignatius, 1987), p. 101.

14. Francis de Sales, quoted in *The Westminster Collection of Christian Quotations*, ed. Martin H. Manser (Louisville: Westminster John Knox, 2001), p. 103.

15. Teresa of Avila, *The Letters of Saint Teresa of Jesus*, vol. 2, ed. Edgar Allison Peers (London: Burns, Oates and Washbourne, 1966), p. 751.

16. Peter Kreeft, *Fundamentals of the Faith: Essays in Christian Apologetics* (San Francisco: Ignatius, 1988), pp. 174–175.

17. *Catechism of the Catholic Church*, second edition (Washington, D.C.: USCCB, 1994), 2473, quoting St. Ignatius of Antioch, *Ad Rom.* 4, 1: SCh 10, 110.

18. Benedict XVI, *The Saints*, Spiritual Thoughts Series (Washington, D.C.: USCCB, 2008), pp. 136–137.

19. Vincent Pallotti, quoted in Joe Paprocki, *The Catechist's Toolbox: How to Thrive as a Religious Education Teacher: Skills, Tips, and Practical Advice You Can Use Today* (Chicago: Loyola, 2007), p. 118.

20. Elizabeth Ann Seton, quoted in *The Flowering of the Soul: A Book of Prayers by Women*, ed. Lucinda Vardey (Toronto: Knopf, 1999), p. 154.

21. Augustine, quoted in Ignatius of Loyola, *The Spiritual Exercises of St. Ignatius* (Whitefish, Mont.: Kessinger, 2005), p. 121.

22. Symeon the New Theologian, quoted in *Writings from the Philokalia*, trans. E. Kadloubovsky (New York: Macmillan, 1955), p. 97.

23. Thérèse of Lisieux, *St. Thérèse of Lisieux*, vol. 1 of *A Treasury of Quotations on the Spiritual Life*, ed. John P. McClernon (San Francisco: Ignatius, 2002), p. 88.

24. Jacques Fesch, quoted in Ann Ball, *Faces of Holiness: Modern Saints in Photos and Words*, vol. 2 (Huntington, Ind.: Our Sunday Visitor, 2001), p. 148.

25. Isidore of Seville, quoted in *The Wisdom of the Saints: An Anthology*, ed. Jill Haak Adels (New York: Oxford University Press, 1989), p. 105.

26. C.S. Lewis, *A Mind Awake; An Anthology of C.S. Lewis*, ed. Clyde S. Kilby (New York: Harcourt Brace Jovanovich, 1980), p. 134.

27. David E. Rosage, *Follow Me: A Pocket Guide to Daily Scriptural Prayer* (Ann Arbor, Mich.: Servant, 1982), p. 210.

28. Julian of Norwich, quoted in *The Flowering of the Soul: A Book of Prayers by Women*, ed. Lucinda Vardey (Toronto: Knopf, 1999), p. 149.

29. *Dei Verbum*, 4. Available at www.vatican.va.

30. Teresa of Calcutta, quoted in Andy Zubko, *Treasury of Spiritual Wisdom: A Collection of 10,000 Powerful Quotations for Transforming Your Life* (New Delhi: Motilal Banarsidass, 2000), p. 424.

31. Fyodor Dostoevsky, quoted in Richard Freeborn, *Dostoevsky* (London: Haus, 2005), p. 40.

32. Irenaeus, quoted in John Bartunek, L.C., *The Better Part: A Christ-Centered Resource for Personal Prayer* (Hamden, Conn.: Circle, 2007), p. 135.

33. Faustina Kowalska, *Diary: Divine Mercy in My Soul*, notebook 1, no. 505 (Stockbridge, Mass.: Marians of the Immaculate Conception, 1999), p. 217.

34. Helen Keller, *The Story of My Life* (Mineola, N.Y.: Dover, 2002), p. 122.

35. John Bosco, quoted in Paul Thigpen, *Last Words: Final Thoughts of Catholic Saints and Sinners* (Cincinnati: Servant, 2006), p. 71.

36. Thérèse of Lisieux, quoted in *The Voice of the Saints: Counsels from the Saints to Bring Comfort and Guidance in Daily Living*, ed. Francis W. Johnston (Rockford, Ill.: TAN, 1986), p. 43.

37. Hannah Flagg Gould, "A Name in the Sand," *Poems Every Child Should Know*, ed. Mary E. Burt (New York: Doubleday, Doran, 1904), p. 256.

38. Thomas Merton, quoted in Thomas J. Tobin, *Without a Doubt: Bringing Faith to Life* (Steubenville, Ohio: Emmaus Road, 2002), p. 95.

39. Ammon, quoted in John Bartunek, L.C., *The Better Part*, p. 389.

40. Augustine, *The Works of St. Augustine* (Hyde Park, N.Y.: Augustine Heritage Institute / New City Press, 1990), p. 229.

41. G.K. Chesterton, quoted in Dale Ahlquist, *G.K. Chesterton: The Apostle of Common Sense* (San Francisco: Ignatius, 2003) p. 62.

42. Thérèse of Lisieux, *St. Thérèse of Lisieux*, vol. 1 of *A Treasury of Quotations on the Spiritual Life*, ed. John P. McClernon (San Francisco: Ignatius, 2002), p. 85.

43. George Basil Hume, O.S.B., *Searching for God* (Leominster, England: Gracewing, 2002), pp. 172–173.

44. Cyprian of Carthage, *Letters 1–81*, trans. Sister Rose Bernard Donna, C.S.J., The Fathers of the Church 51 (Washington, D.C.: Catholic University of America Press, 1965), p. 170.

45. C.S. Lewis, *Mere Christianity: A Revised and Amplified Edition* (New York: HarperCollins, 2001), pp. 140–141.

46. Josemaría Escrivá, *Friends of God: Homilies* (Princeton, N.J.: Scepter, 1977), p. 301.

47. Dronda Bojaxhiu, quoted in *Mother Teresa: Come Be My Light: The Private Writings of the Saint of Calcutta*, ed. Brian Kolodiejchuk, M.C. (New York: Random House, 2007), p. 13.

48. Benedict J. Groeschel, C.F.R., *Quiet Moments with Benedict Groeschel: 120 Daily Readings* (Ann Arbor, Mich.: Servant, 2000), p. 3.

49. Ralph Martin, *The Fulfillment of All Desire: A Guidebook for the Journey to God Based on the Wisdom of the Saints* (Steubenville, Ohio: Emmaus Road, 2006), pp. 170–171.

50. Joseph Pieper, *Faith, Hope, Love* (San Francisco: Ignatius, 1997), p. 85.

51. Thérèse of Lisieux, *St. Thérèse of Lisieux*, vol. 1 of *A Treasury of Quotations on the Spiritual Life*, ed. John P. McClernon (San Francisco: Ignatius, 2002), p. 86.

52. Catherine de Hueck Doherty, *Dearly Beloved: Letters to the Children of My Spirit*, vol. 3 (Combermere, Ont.: Madonna House, 1990), pp. 50–51.

53. John of the Cross, *The Living Flame of Love*, trans. David Lewis (New York: Cosimo, 2007), p. 75.

54. Francis Xavier, quoted in Donna-Marie Cooper O'Boyle, *Catholic Saints Prayer Book: Moments of Inspiration from Your Favorite Saints* (Huntington, Ind.: Our Sunday Visitor, 2008), p. 38.

55. Corrie Ten Boom, *Reflections of Glory: Newly Discovered Meditations* (Grand Rapids: Zondervan, 1999), p. 92.

56. Dietrich Bonhoeffer, *A Testament to Freedom: The Essential Writings of Dietrich Bonhoeffer*, ed. Geoffrey B. Kelly and F. Burton Nelson (New York: HarperCollins, 1995), p. 295.

57. Jean Vanier, *Befriending the Stranger* (Mahwah, N.J.: Paulist, 2010), p. 35.

58. Scott Hahn, *The Lamb's Supper: The Mass as Heaven on Earth* (New York: Doubleday, 1999), p. 128.

59. Thomas à Kempis, quoted in *The Grandeur of God: Selections from Two Thousand Years of Catholic Spiritual Writing*, ed. Joseph Durepos (Chicago: Loyola, 2005), pp. 48–49.

60. Thomas More, quoted in O'Boyle, p. 78.

61. John Paul II, *Lessons for Living*, ed. Joseph Durepos (Chicago: Loyola, 2004), p. 70.

62. Dietrich von Hildebrand, *Confidence in God* (Manchester, N.H.: Sophia Institute, 1997), p. 6.

63. C.S. Lewis, *The Lion, the Witch, and the Wardrobe* (Grand Rapids: Zondervan, 2005), p. 163.

64. Catherine of Siena, quoted in Giuliana Cavallini, O.P., *Catherine of Siena* (New York: Continuum International, 2005), p. 153.

65. Francis de Sales, *Francis de Sales, Jane de Chantal: Letters of Spiritual Direction*, ed. Wendy M. Wright and Joseph F. Power, trans. Péronne Marie Thibert (Mahwah, N.J.: Paulist, 1988), p. 109.

66. Hippolytus, quoted in *Saint of the Day: A Life and Lesson for Each of the 173 Saints of the New Missal*, ed. Leonard Foley, O.F.M. (Cincinnati: St. Anthony Messenger Press, 1975), pp. 52–53.

67. John Paul II, *Lessons for Living*, p. 68.

68. François de Salignac de La Mothe-Fénelon, *Let Go* (New Kensington, Penn.: Whittaker House, 1973), pp. 27–28.

69. Richard John Neuhaus, *Death on a Friday Afternoon: Meditations on the Last Words of Jesus from the Cross* (New York: Basic, 2001), p. 56.

70. Francis de Sales, quoted in Louise Perrotta, ed., *Wisdom from Saints Francis de Sales and Jane de Chantal* (Frederick, Md.: Word Among Us Press, 2000), p. 79.

71. Jean-Pierre de Caussade, *The Sacrament of the Present Moment*, trans. Kitty Muggeridge (San Francisco: HarperSanFrancisco, 1989), p. 28.

72. Thomas Merton, *Thomas Merton, Spiritual Master: The Essential Writings*, ed. Lawrence S. Cunningham (Mahwah, N.J.: Paulist, 1992), p. 307.

73. Benedict XVI, *Holiness Is Always in Season*, ed. Leonardo Sapienza (San Francisco: Ignatius, 2010), p. 42.

74. Thérèse of Lisieux, quoted in Mitch Finley, *What Faith Is Not* (Franklin, Wis.: Sheed and Ward, 2001), p. 44.

75. C.S. Lewis, *A Mind Awake*, p. 138.

76. Augustine, quoted in Thomas Dubay, S.M., *Saints: A Closer Look* (Cincinnati: Servant, 2007), p. 56.

77. Josemaría Escrivá, *Friends of God* (London: Scepter, 1981), pp. 315–316.

78. Thérèse of Lisieux, *The Story of a Soul: The Autobiography of Thérèse of Lisieux*, ed. Mother Agnes of Jesus (Charlotte, N.C.: St. Benedict / TAN, 1997), p. 56.

79. Pierre Teilhard de Chardin, quoted in *The Grandeur of God*, p. 108.

80. Clement XI, quoted in Richard Maffeo, *Lessons Along the Journey* (Maitland, Fla.: Xulon, 2008), p. 33.

81. George Weigel, *The Truth of Catholicism: Ten Controversies Explored* (New York: Cliff Street, 2001), p. 27.

82. John Paul II, *Lessons for Living*, p. 62.

83. Julian of Norwich, *All Will Be Well: Based on the Classic Spirituality of Julian of Norwich*, ed. Richard Chilson (Notre Dame, Ind.: Ave Maria, 1995), pp. 77–79.

84. John Henry Newman, *The Ventures of Faith* (New Rochelle, N.Y.: Scepter, 1981), p. 14.

85. Teresa of Calcutta, *Mother Teresa: Come Be My Light: The Private Writings of the "Saint of Calcutta,"* p. 264.

86. Paul Claudel, quoted in Servais Pinckaers, O.P., *The Sources of Christian Ethics*, trans. Sr. Mary Thomas Noble (Washington, D.C.: Catholic University of America Press, 1995), p. 118.

87. Elizabeth Ann Seton, *Mother Seton: Profile by the Daughters of St. Paul* (Boston: Daughters of St. Paul, 1975), p. 113.

88. Thomas à Kempis, *The Imitation of Christ: A Modern Version Based on the English Translation Made by Richard Whitford Around the Year 1530*, ed. Harold G. Gardiner, S.J. (Garden City, N.Y.: Image, 1955), pp. 84–85.

89. Dietrich von Hildebrand, *Confidence in God*, pp. 69–70.

90. Malcolm Muggeridge, *Jesus, The Man Who Lives* (New York: Harper and Row, 1976), pp. 20, 23.

91. John Paul II, *Lessons for Living*, p. 5.

92. Raniero Cantalamessa, O.F.M., *Faith Which Overcomes the World* (Bannockburn, Ill.: Alpha International, 2005), p. 6.

93. Francis of Assisi, quoted in John Michael Talbot, et al., *The Lessons of St. Francis: How to Bring Simplicity and Spirituality into Your Daily Life* (New York: Plume, 1998), p. 7.

94. Peter Kreeft, *Because God Is Real: Sixteen Questions, One Answer* (San Francisco: Ignatius, 2008), p. 38.

95. Augustine, quoted in *Hold Fast to God: Wisdom from the Early Church*, ed. Jeanne Kun (Ijamsville, Md.: Word Among Us, 2001), p. 12.

96. Thomas à Kempis, *The Imitation of Christ*, p. 112.

97. Richard John Neuhaus, *Death on a Friday Afternoon*, pp. 38–39.

98. Benedict XVI, *Spe Salvi* 10.

99. Basilea Schlink, *Realities: The Miracles of God Experienced Today*, trans. Larry Christenson and William Castell (Grand Rapids: Zondervan, 1966), p. 135.

100. Bede the Venerable, quoted in *The Heart of Catholicism*, p. 347.

101. Teresa of Calcutta, quoted in Dorothy S. Hunt, *Love, A Fruit Always in Season: Daily Meditations From the Words of Mother Teresa of Calcutta* (San Francisco: Ignatius, 1987), p. 66.

102. Paul Johnson, *The Quest for God: A Personal Pilgrimage* (New York: HarperCollins, 1996), pp. 184–185.

103. Walt Whitman, quoted in Donald DeMarco, *The Heart of Virtue: Lessons From Life and Literature Illustrating the Beauty and Value of Moral Character* (San Francisco: Ignatius, 1996), p. 67.

104. George Weigel, *The Truth of Catholicism: Ten Controversies Explored* (New York: Cliff Street Books, 2001), p. 17.

105. Francis de Sales, quoted in *A Treasury of Quotations on the Spiritual Life From the Writings of St. Francis de Sales, Doctor of the Church*, ed. John P. McClernon (San Francisco: Ignatius, 2003), p. 102.

106. Fulton J. Sheen, *Through the Year with Fulton Sheen*, ed. Henry Dieterich (San Francisco: Ignatius, 2003), pp. 9–10.

107. John Vianney, quoted in Robert Ellsberg, *The Saints' Guide to Happiness* (New York: Doubleday, 2005), p. 169.

108. Etty Hillesum, quoted in Henri J.M. Nouwen, *Lifesigns: Intimacy, Fecundity, and Ecstasy in Christian Perspective* (New York: Image, 1986), pp. 112–113.

109. Thomas Howard, *Christ the Tiger: A Postscript to Dogma* (San Francisco: Ignatius, 1990), p. 148.

110. Joseph Bernardin, *The Gift of Peace: Personal Reflections* (Chicago: Loyola, 1997), p. 95.

111. G.K. Chesterton, quoted in Mitch Finley, *What Faith Is Not* (Franklin, Wis.: Sheed and Ward, 2001), p. 58.

112. Dorothy Day, quoted in *The Grandeur of God*, pp. 118–119.

113. Ignatius of Loyola, *Thoughts of St. Ignatius Loyola for Every Day of the Year: From the Scintillae Ignatianae*, ed. Gabriel Havenesi, trans. Alan J. McDougall (New York: Fordham University Press, 2006), p. 44.

114. George MacDonald, *George MacDonald: An Anthology: 365 Readings*, ed. C.S. Lewis (New York: HarperCollins, 2001), p. 85.

115. Henri J. Nouwen, *Jesus: A Gospel*, ed. Michael O'Laughlin (Maryknoll, N.Y.: Orbis, 2001), p. 46.

116. Israel Zolli, quoted in Roy Schoeman, ed., *Honey from the Rock: Sixteen Jews Find the Sweetness of Christ* (San Francisco: Ignatius, 2007), p. 79.

117. Kathleen Norris, *Amazing Grace: A Vocabulary of Faith* (New York: Riverhead, 1998), p. 4.

118. Teresa Benedicta of the Cross, quoted in Waltraud Herbstrith, *Edith Stein: A Biography* (New York: Harper and Row, 1985), p. 36.

119. Michael Scanlan, T.O.R., *What Does God Want? A Practical Guide to Making Decisions* (Huntington, Ind.: Our Sunday Visitor, 1996), p. 86.

120. Caryll Houselander, *A Rocking-horse Catholic: A Caryll Houselander Reader*, ed. Marie Anne Mayeski (Kansas City: Sheed and Ward, 1991), p. 71.

About the Author

Debra Herbeck has worked extensively in youth and women's ministry for the past thirty years. She is the director of the Renewal Ministries School of Catholic Bible Study and the newsletter editor for Renewal Ministries. Her books include *Safely Through the Storm: 120 Reflections on Hope* and *When the Spirit Speaks: Touched by God's Word*, which she coauthored with her husband, Peter.